Slinky and Blinky Skink

Written and photographed by:

Diane Baxter Trapeni

ISBN: 9798639221675

Keep an eye out for these other exciting titles:

Nellie the Nibbler

Alice the Guinea Pig

Penny the Python

Jeremiah, a Song Bird

Vincent

Hubert

Phil Harmonic

Jeff Sticks up for his Buddies

Cord, Glue and 8 Screws

A Three Piggie Circus

DEDICATION

To my beautiful nieces, Lauren, Nicole and Jessica, who look at life differently and make me very happy. I love you girls so much!

DMBT

Slinky is a crocodile Skink. What's a Skink, you ask? Well, I can tell you what he's NOT! He's NOT a snake, but he resembles one. He's NOT a fish but he can swim through sand.

He's not a frog but he can wriggle through water…
…and he's not a sprinter but he can undulate through the underbrush easily and with great speed!

Can you see him in your mind yet? NO? Let's see.
In Florida he's called a Sand Skink.
In the deserts of the Middle East, he's called a Sand Fish.

In Australia, he is called a Land Mullet! In Europe, he's a Slow Worm!
(He's not SLOW and he's NOT a WORM!).
So I think you're beginning to see Slinky's problem. Everyone knows of him but no one really knows him.

Slinky is spotted here and there but he's not here, he's there! You See? He gets blamed for things he couldn't possibly do. He is FAST but he doesn't fly so how could he have done it? So, NO, he did not eat your cousin in Florida!
He's in Australia! Look at a map. See?

Have you ever been blamed for something you didn't do and no one believed you? Well, I believe you because it happens to me all the time!
But that's another story...

Slinky said he only wishes he had a blue tongue, like cousin, Kinky Skink.
Then…If he gets blamed again for something he DIDN'T DO, he'd just stick out his tongue at them and they'd say, "Oh…it wasn't him!"

Monte the Moniker

Slinky and Blinky are afraid. A "dragon" just moved into the neighborhood.
 He is a muscular Monitor.
He looks mean and hungry…and guess what he eats???? SKINKS!!!

Monte is big. Monte is muscular...

He can bench press both of us at the same time! Yes!

He always looks hungry. Yes!

His neighbors (US) look delicious. Yes!

But Montgomery is trying something new. He wants to polish other skills besides hunting.

He kind of likes his dragon costume...a LOT! He has been asked to be in a famous Halloween Parade and he only moved in 3 days ago!!! News travels fast in this small town! Imagine...a job already.
This could turn into something big!

The skinks, on the other hand, are beside themselves in TERROR!!! They have seen his tongue. They don't dare go outside. They'll starve if this keeps up!!! As the 2 huddled and shook in the middle of their living room floor, the doorbell rang. It was Slinky's turn to answer it. Without even peeking out the blinds, he opened the door. To his horror, there stood Monte.

Monte looked at Slinky. Slinky stared at Monte while rooted to the spot. His heart was racing and he felt faint. No one moved.

"Slinky" yelled Blinky. "Who is it?" Slinky blinked but was too scared to make a sound. He tried but nothing came out!

Monte tried to introduce himself but Slinky hit his head hard on the floor when he fainted. Blinky ran to the door to see what happened and stopped dead. "You killed him?" "My brother is dead?" Blinky panicked. He went directly from scared to MAD!!! He attacked Monte even though Monte was 8 feet long and 200 pounds!

Monte held him back by placing his huge paw on Blinky's head while Blinky continued to try to punch, scratch and kick him.

Slinky came to and saw Blinky in trouble.

He jumped up to try to save his baby brother.

What a horrific misunderstanding!!!

Montgomery just came over to introduce himself to his new neighbors and they thought they were dinner!!! After a few more minutes of this, the 2 skinks tired. Monte let them go and they both fell down…breathing hard. Monte reached down, shook their hands, introduced himself and sat on a tiny couch.
(The couch is no more!)

Slinky began to cry.

He was so relieved.

After apologizing, they decided to start over.

Sometimes you imagine a problem where

there isn't one. Give everyone a chance

before you judge.

The End

(of prejudging.)

Keep an eye out for these other exciting Children's Books:

Penny the Enormous Python

Floyd the Colorful Chameleon

Francesca the Tropical Red-eyed Green Frog

Joe's Got Spots

Merrill the Squirrel and Jen the Hen:

Part 6 Brittany's Back!!!

Sydney (Cat)

Alice the Guinea Pig

Frances, a Gifted Frog for Sure!

Saffire. (Butterfly)

Serendipity. (Fish)

Jeremiah, the Song Bird

Christmas at the Castle

We are proud to introduce:

Inky and Rambo

Rambo's life was fun and exciting much like our lives are but Inky was bored, lonely, and most of all, sad…He needed to go home so he practiced and plotted until…Well, find out for yourselves boys and girls how strong a bond LOVE is! Enjoy!

About the TrapStone LLC: Owner and Author…

My name is Miss Diane. I taught for 42 years and have read thousands of books aloud to children.

I enjoyed that so much, I decided to write and illustrate books for you myself.

Enjoy!!!

Ken Stone Sr. is a computer programmer and a business partner extraordinaire. He put my words, pictures and computer magic together so you could meet, Slinky and Blinky Skink.

www.ingramcontent.com/pod-product-compliance
Lightning Source LLC
Chambersburg PA
CBHW042132110726
48006CB00003B/853